MW01620465

Written by Mari Tzikas Suarez

Illustrated by Nuri Amanatullah

ISBN: 978-0-578-48451-8

Printed in PRC

www.eieiart.com

@eieiartbook

What's happenin'? I'm Young MacDonald. Call me Mac. My grandfather, Old MacDonald, was pretty famous in his "hay" day. Maybe you've heard of him?

Growing up on the farm, I learned how to plow like a pro
and make the best milkshakes of all time.

But I was not prepared to inherit the farm!
What was Gramps thinking leaving me in charge?

Without him here, the swine got whiny, the chicken started flip-flappin' out, and I think I heard the cow say, "BOOOOO" instead of, "MOOOOO." No amount of milkshakes could make me feel better, either.

So I did what I had to. I packed up my herd and headed to...

...the big city.

The pig went hog wild. The chicken became so flip-flappin' happy!
And I'm pretty sure I heard the cow say, "WAHOOOOO!"

With farm life behind us, I gave the animals a bale of paper, a bushel of brushes, and a truckload of paints and told them to let their creativity roam free.
Of course, everyone needed new nicknames, too.

The colors! The patterns! The imagination! You shoulda seen the work coming outta here. This place was hoppin'.

But then Porkcasso stole all the blue paints.

Quackson Pollock made a mess of the joint.

Da Vin-chick teased Mo-neigh for his blurry work.

Salvadog Dalí became quite boisterous
and injured Sniffcent van Gogh's ear.

Bahhhtticelli and Andy Warhoof kept eating each other's paintings.

And Frida Cowlo? All the chaos made her so cranky that
she started to really chap *my* hide.

The egos! The attitude! The ruffled feathers!

It was as if everyone was raised in a barn.

So I rolled up my sleeves and tried to do what Gramps would have done.

A grass patch here.

A fence up there.

Here a coop.

There a trough.

Everywhere some fresh air...and milkshakes!

And you know what? It worked! I guess there's a little farmer in me after all...and I kinda dig it!

Gramps would love seeing us live it up like this.

Luckily, he has a pretty good view.

SALVADOG DALI

SNIFFCENT VAN GOGH

QUACKSON POLLOCK

MO-NEIGH

And back at the farm? Things are goin' just fine.
We opened a gallery, and it's making tons of moo-la.

"A-graze-ing!"

"Egg-cellent!"

"Udderly inspiring!"

THE
FARM HAUS

I may not be good at farming, but I do have a knack for nicknames. Here's a little background on the artists that inspired the animals' artist identities.

Sandro Botticelli (1445-1510) led the way during the Early Renaissance era in Florence, Italy, with his biblical- and mythological-inspired masterpieces.
Fun Mac Fact: A crater on the planet Mercury is named after him.

Salvador Dalí (1904-1989) was a Spanish Surrealist painter who fancied bizarre symbols, like melting clocks, eggs, and elephants.
Fun Mac Fact: His signature look included a long, black cape and a long, black mustache.

Leonardo da Vinci (1452-1519) did it ALL! During the Italian Renaissance, he was a master of the arts (painting, sculpting, music) and sciences (mathematics, anatomy, astronomy).
Fun Mac Fact: He wrote backwards in his notebooks, so you could only properly read them if you held the pages up to a mirror.

Vincent van Gogh (1853-1890) was part of the French Post-Impressionist movement and is famous for his landscape, still life, and portrait paintings.
Fun Mac Fact: In a fit of madness, he chopped his left ear off. (Ouch!)

Frida Kahlo (1907-1954) started painting as a teen while recovering from a bus accident. She's beloved for her vibrant self-portraits and bold eyebrows. **Fun Mac Fact:** At her home, La Casa Azul, in Mexico City, Mexico, she had spider monkeys, Mexican hairless dogs, and parrots as pets.

Claude Monet (1840-1926) founded Impressionism—a style that uses lots of small brushstrokes—with his paintings of the French countryside. **Fun Mac Fact:** You can visit his home and gardens in Giverny, France, and see the sites of his most famous paintings!

Pablo Picasso (1881-1973) was a Spanish painter, sculptor, and poet (to name a few things) who lived in Paris, France, and helped invent Cubism. **Fun Mac Fact:** His first word was "piz," a shortened version of the Spanish word for pencil, "lápiz." Coincidence? I don't think so!

Jackson Pollock (1912-1956) wowed the art world in the late 1940s with his "drip" technique—which looks a lot like splatter painting. **Fun Mac Fact:** Pollock converted a barn on his property into an art studio. Smart guy!

Andy Warhol (1928-1987) was an American Pop artist and party boy and is legendary for his colorful screen prints of soup cans, celebrities, and more. **Fun Mac Fact:** Just like me, he had his own artist's loft in New York City. It was called The Factory.